The Christmas

Conversation

Piece

By Bret Nicholaus and Paul Lowrie

The Conversation Piece
The Christmas Conversation Piece

The Christmas Conversation Piece

*Creative Questions
to Illuminate
the Holidays*

**Bret Nicholaus and
Paul Lowrie**

Ballantine Books   New York

This book is dedicated to the following people:

My wife and best friend, Christina, for her constant love.

My mom, Lorrie, who always, *always* made the house a home and who taught me more about how to live than she'll ever know.

My late dad, Alan, and my late grandfathers, David Raymond Johnson and Herbert Nicholaus, all three of whom were loved and respected by all who were fortunate enough to know them.

—B. N.

My mom, Janice, and my dad, Donald, for unconditionally helping me pursue my seemingly impractical dreams.

My sisters, Anita and Becky, for the little ways they enrich my life.

—P. L.

Acknowledgments

We would mutually like to thank

Randy Bray, for his never-ending support and help on this book.

Joe Durepos, a great literary agent and a wonderful person as well.

Everyone at Ballantine Books who believed in this project from the very beginning.

Our Lord, Jesus Christ, who came down from heaven at Christmas and rose victorious over death at Easter.

Welcome

Christmas . . . Ask 50 different people what it means and you're likely to get a list of responses as varied as the gifts under the tree. Some might say it's the time of year when winter lays its first white blanket on a barren ground. Others will tell you it's the time when giving becomes a far greater joy than receiving. And for yet others, the season is defined by songs about mangers and a hallelujah chorus or two. While each of us may attach a meaning to Christmas peculiar to our own beliefs and desires, most of us would ultimately agree that much of Christmas's meaning is to be found in the gathering together of people, whether they be new acquaintances, old friends, or much-loved family.

It is at these Christmas gatherings, big and small, that a common little word called "conversation" takes on uncommon importance, that typical discussions of politics and careers yield a little to conversations about goodwill and great memories. We reminisce with Grandpa as logs crackle in the fireplace; we chat with our children around a freshly cut tree; we have heartwarming talks with friends at holiday dinners and share hearty laughs with colleagues around the corporate punch bowl. It would be difficult to argue that any other time of the year affords so many great opportunities to engage in conversation. With this thought in mind, *The Christmas Conversation Piece* was created.

The purpose of this book is to enhance all your Christmas conversations and draw you closer to friends and family through the use of creative and entertaining questions. Since you probably have never thought about many of the questions in this collection, you will also be drawn closer to your own thoughts, feelings, and ideas about this joyous season. Between questions about favorite carols and favorite ornaments, new gift wrapping techniques and old St. Nick, you'll never be at a loss for words. In fact, you'll find questions in here dealing with everything from tropical islands to the president of the United States—with the holiday season always at the heart of the question!

It is our hope that this book will add a new element of fun and enthusiasm to your holiday discussions while helping each one of us to rediscover Christmas, with all the enchanting nuances it has to offer. And so, from both of us, "Merry Christmas to all and to all . . . a good conversation!"

Bret Nicholaus

Paul Lowrie

1

In your opinion, what would the ultimate winter wonderland look like?

2

You're the author of a new Christmas novel that you hope will one day become a classic. What would you choose as the setting for your Christmas story?

3

What is your favorite Christmas scent?

4

What do you think is the most enjoyable thing to do in the snow?

5

If you were a photographer who was given the chance to go back in history to capture a Christmas photograph, where would you go and what year would it be?

6

Regardless of its monetary value, what is the single most meaningful Christmas gift you've ever received?

7

Someone has graciously offered to make you and your entire family a Christmas quilt. It will be made up of many quilt squares, each one representing a different family member. What specific design or image would you want on your square?

8

If time were not a concern and you had plenty of money, how would you decorate the outside of your home?

9

If, like Santa, you could take a night flight in a sleigh over any city in the world, which city would you choose?

10

Suppose that a new fad was to wrap your gifts in anything other than wrapping paper. With what would you wrap your presents?

11

What ingredients go into your favorite Christmas drink or beverage?

12

Candy canes, of course, are the traditional candy of Christmas. If you could have your way, what would be the official candy of Christmas?

13

On a scale of one to ten (with one being in perfect order and ten being an intertwined, out-of-control mess), how tangled are your Christmas lights when you first take them out each year?

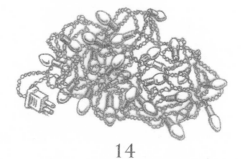

14

You've been chosen to host a sensational Christmas celebration on TV. What three guests (living or deceased) would you have on the show to make it the best Christmas special ever?

15

You have a beautiful 50-foot pine tree in your front yard that you are allowed to decorate with only one color of lights. Which color would you choose?

16

When was the last time you can remember making an angel in the snow? If it's been awhile—and you have snow—go out and do it just for fun!

17

Have you ever given someone a fruitcake for Christmas? Approximately how many fruitcakes over the years do you think you've received?

18

You are a painter and have just been commissioned to do a large oil-on-canvas painting that depicts something about the holiday season. What scene would you choose to paint?

19

If you were one of the three kings visiting the Bethlehem baby in *today's* world, what would you bring as a gift?

20

If you were designing a brand-new outfit for old St. Nick, what would it look like?

21

Which of the following three events would you most enjoy attending during the holiday season: a stage production of Dickens's *A Christmas Carol*, a choral concert of Handel's *Messiah*, or a performance of Tchaikovsky's ballet *The Nutcracker*?

22

If you could write a sequel to any Christmas movie ever produced, which one would you choose and what would the plot be?

23

If you were creating the ultimate gingerbread house, what unique features would it have?

24

In what order do you generally accessorize your tree? (Examples: Star first or last, ornaments before lights or lights before ornaments?)

25

If you could have any kind of tree besides the standard evergreen as your Christmas tree, what type would you choose?

26

What is the longest period of time you've ever left your tree up after Christmas?

27

Regardless of your gender, which role in a live nativity scene do you think you're best cut out for?

28

Suppose you have a 50-gallon aquarium in your home. How will you creatively decorate it for the fish this holiday season?

29

Of course, red and green are the traditional colors of Christmas. What two other colors do you think could—or should—become the standard for the season?

30

If you were going to be Santa Claus for a Christmas Eve, what one amenity or convenience factor would you insist that your sleigh feature?

31

What type of design or pattern on wrapping paper would definitely catch your eye?

32

You're involved in a gift exchange at work where the only thing you know about the intended recipient is that he/she is the same sex as you. Your spending cap is $15; what would you buy as the gift?

33

Do you prefer blinking or nonblinking Christmas lights?

34

Out of all the musical instruments, which one do you think is the most appropriate for the Christmas season?

35

If you had a miniature Christmas village set up in your home, what shop, building, or other object would be the most prominently displayed in your little town?

36

If you were hosting an all-expenses-paid Christmas party for children at an orphanage, what specific thing would you be sure to do to make it a Christmas the children would never forget?

37

Besides the golden rings, which gift from "The Twelve Days of Christmas" would you be most interested in receiving?

38

In your opinion, how many inches (if any) would be the ideal accumulation of snow for a white Christmas?

39

At Christmastime, which do you *honestly* enjoy more—giving or receiving?

40

You're in charge of developing a brand-new sport—a Christmas sport. The season begins on Thanksgiving and ends on December 25. What is your new Christmas sport going to be?

41

This year, would you rather spend Christmas at a penthouse in the city or at a cottage in the country?

42

If you were given 1,000 fresh poinsettia plants, what would you do with them? Be specific.

43

What is the first Christmas you can remember? What specific aspects of it do you recall?

44

Do you have any ethnic or ancestral traditions that you honor during the Christmas season?

45

If you had to move the celebration of Christmas from December 25 to a new date, where on the calendar would you put it?

46

In your opinion, what word(s) would best complete the following phrase: " 'Tis the season to be . . ."?

47

As the Christmas season draws near, what song is it that you can't wait to hear?

48

What particular holiday food do you enjoy the most?

49

In your opinion, what would be the ideal temperature for Christmas Day?

50

Without looking in your ornament storage box, approximately how many ornaments could you describe from memory?

51

Everyone at the office has been asked to place an ornament on the company Christmas tree that best represents him/herself. What would your ornament look like?

52

If you could spend Christmas in any European country, which one would you choose?

53

If you were asked to choose four songs for a Christmas medley, which songs would you pick?

54

In your opinion, how would an angelic choir look, and how would it sound? Be as specific as you can.

55

For you, what is the most discouraging aspect of the Christmas season?

56

As a curious child, did you ever shake gifts under the tree to try and figure out what you were getting? Do you still shake (or subtly lift) packages before Christmas?

57

Which particular event or aspect of the Christmas season do you look forward to most of all?

58

You must choose between Christmas caroling for a children's hospital or for a convalescent home. Which one would you choose, and what reason would you give to defend your choice?

59

If you had written the story, what type of animal would be pulling Santa's sleigh?

60

What is your favorite Christmas sound?

61

If you won $5,000 the week before Christmas, where do you think you'd go for a Christmas vacation?

62

This year, what is the most important thing on your Christmas list?

63

If you own a pet, does it have its own stocking? Does it get Christmas gifts along with everyone else?

64

If snow could fall in any flavor, what flavor would you choose?

65

If an ice company offered to carve a large ice sculpture for you, what object would you want them to carve?

66

What makes a Christmas gift really special to you?

67

If you could somehow give one of the following intangible gifts to every person living in the world, which one would you choose—hope, joy, love, or peace?

68

If you were creating a movie about toys coming to life, which toy would be your main character?

69

What is the longest line you can remember waiting in during the Christmas season?

If you were given thousands of dollars to develop an incredible electric train layout that would run at the base of a huge Christmas tree in a mall, what might it look like upon completion?

Approximately how many parties do you attend during the typical Christmas season?

72

If you had outstanding promotion and distribution working behind you, what brand-new toy—children's or adults'—would you create and introduce?

73

What is the oldest ornament on your Christmas tree?

74

Where does Santa summer?

75

If you could Christmas shop until you drop in any one store, which store would you choose?

76

When does it *really* start feeling like Christmas to you?

77

In terms of overall size, how large (or small) do you envision Santa's workshop?

78

When you think of the holiday season in New York City, what particular scene or image do you picture first?

79

If you were in charge of hiring a department store Santa, what quality or ability above all others would you look for in the applicants?

80

In which of the following locations would you most enjoy spending Christmas— Colorado, Tennessee, or Vermont?

81

If you were going to go out for dinner on Christmas Day, would you tip more than usual since the waiter or waitress is having to work on the holiday?

82

How many people do you know named Joseph? How many people do you know named Mary?

83

Were you ever in a Christmas pageant? If so, what part did you play?

84

According to the biblical Christmas story, Mary was very surprised to learn that she would be bearing the son of God. What is the best Christmas surprise that you've ever had?

85

Everyone has a favorite Christmas story or experience that he/she loves to share. What's yours?

86

If you had the money to develop the ultimate fireplace, what would it look like?

87

How many new words can you derive from the word *Christmas*? You need not use all the letters. (Example: The word *his*.)

88

Do you have a traditional Christmas dinner that you prepare year after year? If so, what is it?

89

How do you think you would react if *you* were visited by an angel?

90

If, as the winner of a Christmas contest, you were given five minutes in one of the following three departments to haul away as many items as you could physically carry out the door, which department would you choose—consumer electronics, home furnishings and accessories, or sports equipment and attire? (Assume that you cannot solicit the help of a salesperson.)

91

If you were hosting a small group of people for a Christmas party and had to choose something other than showing a movie for the entertainment, what would you choose?

92

Approximately how many Christmas cards do you send out each year?

93

Have you ever cut down your own Christmas tree? If you had a convenient opportunity to do so, would you?

94

In terms of height, shape, and type, what would you consider the ideal Christmas tree?

95

What do you typically do the day after Christmas?

96

If an acquaintance wanted to spend about $15 on a gift for you, what would you suggest that he/she buy?

97

If you could dress up a snowman as someone famous, who would it look like?

98

It's a *Wonderful Life*, *Miracle on 34th Street*, or *White Christmas*—which one would get your vote for the best classic Christmas movie?

99

If you had a child born on Christmas Day and had to give him/her a name that related to Christmas, what name would you choose? (Example: *Holly* for a girl.)

100

If you were going to create and market a holiday cologne or perfume, what would you choose for the fragrance?

101

Given the choice, would you rather host people at your place for Christmas or travel and spend the holiday at someone else's home?

102

If you could indulge in only one type of cookie this holiday season, which cookie would you be eating a lot of?

103

If, through the use of a time machine, you could travel back in time to briefly revisit any Christmas moment in your life, which one would you choose?

104

If you had to write a Christmas greeting no more than ten words in length that would be printed on 100,000 Christmas cards, what would it be?

105

A large snowman has been built in a popular city park; it is your job to supply the hat for his head. What hat would you choose to make this snowman unique?

106

Approximately how many dozens of cookies do you bake during a typical Christmas season? Would you like to guess at how many you eat during the season?

107

If you could go anywhere at all to reflect and meditate on the meaning of Christmas, where would you go?

108

What has been your worst holiday travel dilemma/experience to date?

109

What gift have you wanted for years, but still haven't received?

110

In your opinion, what is the most timeless toy?

111

What's the most creative way you can think of to decorate your car for Christmas?

112

When does your family traditionally open gifts?

113

If you could decorate any store's window for the Christmas season, which one would you choose?

114

Many snow globes feature something other than snow that falls (e.g., hundreds of little, white bones in a globe featuring a dog). What do you think would be most interesting to have falling inside a snow globe?

115

What is your all-time biggest Christmas shopping disaster?

116

Suppose that a friend or relative gives you a gift that he/she is personally very excited to have given. You, on the other hand, either have no use for it or simply don't like it. How would you react to the giver? Would you pretend that you like it? Would you try to exchange it for cash or for another item?

117

If you could invite any famous person to your house for Christmas dinner, whom would you invite?

118

If you could have two front-row tickets for any musical event this Christmas, what or whom would you most like to hear?

119

Of all your friends and family members, which person do you think is best suited to play the part of Santa Claus?

120

If you were to file a complaint with the Better Christmas Bureau, what would your complaint be?

121

If you were playing Name That Tune, which Christmas song do you think you could identify in the least number of notes? Think carefully!

122

If someone wanted to give you a $100 gift certificate for Christmas, what store would you want it to be from?

123

If you could go back in American history to experience Christmas dinner and conversation with a typical family of that day, which of the following years would you want to go back to?

a. 1620, the year the *Mayflower* arrived
b. 1787, the year the Constitution was signed
c. 1863, midway through the American Civil War
d. 1899, the turn of the century

124

If you were to open up a cozy, little Christmas shop, what Christmas product would be your main draw?

125

If you were the coordinator in charge of staging a nationwide Christmas event, one in which every American theoretically could participate, what would this grand event be?

126

A candy cane company, which lost sales last year to the chocolate market, has asked you to create a catchy slogan that positions candy canes as the superior candy. What will your slogan be? Take a few minutes and have some fun with this one!

127

What aspect of preparing for Christmas do you like the most?

128

Suppose that a major motion-picture company was producing a Christmas movie about a real-life Grinch. What actor or actress do you think would be best suited to play the leading role?

129

By the time Christmas actually arrives, many of us are too tired to enjoy it. Approximately when—between Thanksgiving and December 25—does your holiday spirit peak?

130

Suppose you could have any gift in the world this Christmas, regardless of cost, provided it could fit in the trunk of a mid-sized car. What would you want?

131

Have you ever worked in retail sales during the holiday season? If so, what was your most interesting experience?

132

S uppose that there was a nationwide shortage of Christmas trees and prices went through the roof. Assuming that artificial trees are not an option, what is the absolute most you'd be willing to pay for a real tree?

133

I f you were going to write an editorial column for your city's newspaper covering any Christmas topic of your choice, what would you write about?

134

If you could create the perfect hill for sledding, what would it look like? Be specific.

135

If Frosty the Snowman really did come to life for a day, what one national attraction or tourist site would you encourage him to see before he melted away?

136

No other time of the year affords such a great opportunity to enjoy good food and drink. In your opinion, what is the best taste the Christmas season has to offer?

137

A major theme of the Christmas season is peace on earth. For whatever your reason, what do you consider the most peaceful place on earth?

138

What aspect of preparing for Christmas do you like the least?

139

What would you choose as an international symbol for the word *Christmas*?

140

What is your favorite Christmas phrase, quote, or verse?

141

If you were the one delivering gifts to all the world's children, what would you consider the perfect temperature for your all-night sleigh flight around the earth?

142

How likely are you to run out of wrapping paper before you finish wrapping all your gifts? Do you have a lot of leftover paper at the end of the season?

143

If luck favored you and you won $100,000 during the holiday season, what percent of your winnings (if any) do you think you'd give away to others?

144

What is your favorite Christmas decoration in your home? (The Christmas tree doesn't count!)

145

If you were a movie producer, which of the following three cities would you choose as the setting for a new Christmas movie—New York, Denver, or Minneapolis?

146

Whose televised Christmas special do you anticipate the most each year?

147

If it were socially acceptable for you to play with any children's toy, with which toy would you be spending a lot of time?

148

If you were blind, but miraculously had the chance to see for 24 hours during one holiday of the year, would you necessarily choose Christmas? If not, which holiday would you most want to see?

149

If you could de-commercialize Christmas, what is the first change you would make?

150

At what age do you think children are the cutest to watch at Christmas?

151

Which state in our country do you find the most difficult to associate with the Christmas season?

152

Each year Easter falls at a slightly different time on the calendar. How would you feel if Christmas followed a similar pattern, falling at a different time each year between Thanksgiving and New Year's?

153

If you were in charge of developing a town that would be the most peaceful place to live on earth, which particular features would characterize it?

154

Have you ever purposely stood under mistletoe with the hope of being kissed by someone? Have you ever unknowingly stood under mistletoe and been kissed by someone?

155

For the perfect romantic evening during the holiday season, where would you most want to go?

156

Regardless of the electric bill, what man-made or natural object would you most like to see strung or outlined with Christmas lights?

157

During the Christmas season, would you be more likely to give money to a certain charity or to a specific individual in need?

158

What magazine and/or catalog's Christmas issue is an absolute "must read" for you?

159

What would be the ideal way for you to spend Christmas Eve?

160

If any Christmas song were to bring you to tears, which one would it be?

161

If you had to ascribe an age to Santa Claus based on how old you think he looks, what age would you give him?

162

Suppose you have just arrived from another planet and are getting your first glimpse of this thing called Christmas. Having never heard of Christmas or experienced it in any way, what do you think you would find most fascinating about it?

163

According to the biblical Christmas story, the three kings followed a star and ultimately found the baby Jesus. What is the greatest thing, tangible or intangible, that *you've* ever found?

164

Which of the following, if it were completely and permanently removed from the holiday season, would be the most difficult for you to get along without—Christmas lights, Christmas music, or Christmas parties? Think carefully!

165

If you were asked to concoct a Christmas dessert for a five-star restaurant, what would the dessert be?

166

If you were on a committee assigned to decorating the world's largest Christmas tree, what suggestions would you have for the adorning of the tree?

167

What is one Christmas tradition that you have not yet started but that you think would be fun to begin?

168

What Christmas object in your home has the most sentimental value?

169

What Christmas song drives you nuts?

170

If you had the opportunity to take a Christmas ride down and around Chicago's famous Michigan Avenue, would you rather take the tour in one of the popular horse-drawn carriages or in a luxurious white stretch limousine?

171

During the holiday season, what specific aspect of being a young child do you miss the most?

172

Have you ever kept track of how much money you spend in one year directly related to Christmas (e.g., gifts, entertaining, and the like)?

173

What is one of the simple joys of Christmas that you like to savor to the fullest?

174

If you had a great voice and could record a Christmas duet with any famous singer, whom would you choose as your singing partner?

175

What is your favorite holiday of the entire year?

176

For the sake of comparison, you've been asked to stage two scenes of the American family and household at Christmas—one scene is this year, the other scene is 30 years ago. What differences would people see between the two? Be specific.

177

On a scale of one to ten (with one being very relaxing and ten being very stressful), how stressful is the holiday season for you?

178

If you could somehow change the number of days in the month of December, would you make the month longer or shorter, and by how many days?

179

If you were Santa Claus, what food and beverage would you want children to leave for you?

180

If you could get anyone in the world to be the keynote speaker for a large Christmas dinner you're coordinating, whom would you choose?

181

If you were one of three judges in charge of selecting the best small-town Christmas in the United States, what particular criterion would be most important in your decision?

182

If you were involved in a progressive holiday dinner, for which course would you want to be responsible—hors d'oeuvres, soup, salad, main course, or dessert?

183

Do you ever listen to Christmas music out of season (e.g., in the middle of summer)?

184

If keeping the laughs going at your Christmas party was a primary concern, whom would you be sure to invite out of all your friends?

185

If you were asked to write a dictionary definition for the word *Christmas*, how would you define it in 20 words or less?

186

If you could have any Christmas antique, what would you choose?

187

If you could somehow "jump into" any Christmas carol or song and actually experience what the lyrics say, which song would you choose?

188

If you were the owner of a bed-and-breakfast inn, what would you do to make the Christmas season special for your guests?

189

What is one thing you've always wanted to do during the holiday season, but haven't done thus far?

190

If you were going to establish a U.S. mailing address for Santa Claus, which city and state do you think would be most appropriate?

191

During the rush of the Christmas season, which chore, activity, or discipline do you tend to neglect the most?

192

If you were to receive a tin of all the same kind of nut, would you want it to contain cashews, filberts, pecans, or pistachios?

193

If you could make a wish upon a Christmas star, what would you wish for?

194

You're in charge of developing a planned community called Christmas City. What are some of the plans on the drawing board that keep with the Christmas theme?

195

If you could spend Christmas Day with any TV family, past or present, with which family would you choose to celebrate? (Example: The Bunkers.)

196

If Christmas is a state of mind, what attitude or attribute above all others need one possess in order to maintain a Christmas state of mind all year long?

197

Which winter/holiday Currier and Ives print comes to your mind first?

198

Other than simply giving a small check or cash gift, what act of kindness do you think would be nice to do for an individual in need this Christmas season?

199

Besides the reindeer, which animal(s) do you associate the most with the Christmas season?

200

You have two options for where you can spend Christmas: a ski resort in the mountains or a tropical resort on a Caribbean island. Which would you choose?

201

If you or your family could have a
Christmas photograph taken anywhere in
the world, where would you want to have the
picture taken? (Assume the photo will be sent
out in all your Christmas cards.)

202

If you were the wedding coordinator in
charge of a Christmas wedding, what is
one Christmas detail that you would want to
incorporate into the big day?

203

If you had to replace the customary Christmas tree with a new Christmas conversation piece, what would become its replacement?

204

If a baker offered to bake you one specific treat for Christmas, what would you choose?

205

If this Christmas you could be instantly transported to London's St. Paul's Cathedral to hear any one musical work or composition, what would you most want to hear? (It needn't have a Christmas theme.)

206

How long before Christmas do you traditionally begin shopping for gifts?

207

If you were president of the United States, what nonmonetary act of goodwill would you want the country to see you performing?

208

If you could take a how-to course in anything related to the Christmas season, in what course would you want to enroll?

209

If you got a puppy or kitten for Christmas and had to name it after one of the nine reindeer—Dasher, Dancer, Prancer, Vixen, Comet, Cupid, Donner, Blitzen, or Rudolph—what would you name it?

210

He's making a list and checking it twice. On a scale of one to ten (with one being very naughty and ten being very nice), how naughty or nice have you been this year?

There are two gifts under the tree with your name on them, but you may only choose one. One gift is in a three-inch-square box, the other is in a three-foot-square box. The monetary value of both gifts is exactly the same; which one will you choose? (No fair shaking!)

212

Take a few moments and paint a picture of the word *December* in your mind's eye. What does it look like? Describe it vividly!

213

In that famous Christmas song, all the child wants is his two front teeth. If you could receive any physical feature or attribute this Christmas, what would you ask for?

214

What is the most unusual and/or unique Christmas tradition you've ever heard of?

215

Which particular job would you least like to have around the holiday season?

216

In how many different languages can you say "Merry Christmas"?

217

If you could see one snowfall in a color other than white, what color would you want it to be?

218

If you were going to make a Christmas wreath out of something other than pine boughs, what would you use to make your wreath truly unique?

219

Around Christmastime there really does seem to be a special feeling in the air. What particular feeling above all others does Christmas evoke in you?

220

In that famous Christmas poem, the house is so quiet the night before Christmas that not even a mouse is stirring. What is the usual atmosphere in your house the night before Christmas?

221

If you could decorate any famous building for Christmas (inside and outside), which building would you choose?

222

What's your favorite holiday commercial or advertisement?

223

If any of our past presidents—living or deceased—could be brought back for a day to deliver a Christmas address to the nation, whose speech would you be most interested in hearing?

224

If a child asked you what causes Rudolph's nose to glow, what would your response be?

225

As a late-night talk-show host, you must book a guest for your December 23 show who is highly relevant to the Christmas season. Whom would you choose as the guest? (The person does not have to be famous.)

226

Which Christmas song's lyrics have you memorized more completely than any other?

227

If you were to start a snow globe collection around a certain theme, what would the theme be?

228

Whan Christmas object(s) do you think would be the most eye-catching if it were printed on a tie?

229

Are you more likely to give someone a gift that they really *want* or a gift that you think they really *need*?

230

Which of the following three holidays do you enjoy the most, and which do you enjoy the least—Thanksgiving Day, Christmas Day, or New Year's Day?

231

If you were going to create and market an ice cream especially for the Christmas season, what would it be like?

232

If you had to describe your personality in terms of a Christmas object, which object would you choose? (Example: A snow globe, if you're the type who gets "shaken up" easily.)

233

If you could walk down a path that would lead you into an experience of perfect Christmas joy and bliss, to what specific experience would you most want to be led?

234

If you could create a new holiday by blending Christmas traditions with those of another established holiday, which two special days would you combine?

235

If you were going to decorate a Christmas tree outdoors for the birds and animals, what type of edibles would you hang from the tree?

236

How many words beginning with the letter *C* can you think of that relate directly to the Christmas season? (Example: Candle.)

237

If you were given one pound of fresh cranberries, what would you do with them?

238

Which job or occupation do you think would be the most rewarding around the holiday season?

239

In your opinion, do the large crowds of people at Christmastime add or detract from the overall shopping experience?

240

When the excitement of Christmas and New Year's is over, what is the next big day that you begin to anticipate?

241

What is the most creative way you can think of to present an engagement ring during the holidays?

242

If all the Christmas gifts you gave away this year had to be homemade by you, what would you be most likely to make?

243

What is the most interesting piece of Christmas trivia that you know?

You must add a new pair of reindeer to Santa's sleigh-pulling team (the load's a little heavier this year). What would you name the two newcomers?

Have you ever written clues on gift tags to give the recipient "a sneak preview" as to what's inside? (Example: "This gift serves you right," if you're giving a tennis raquet.)

246

What street in your city or town do you most like to walk down during the Christmas season?

247

What has been the greatest blessing in your life since last Christmas?

248

Do you know who Clement Clarke Moore was?

249

What Christmas movie that you haven't seen for years are you yearning to see again?

250

Which particular aspect of the biblical Christmas account are you most interested in?

251

If fallen snow had a scent, what scent would you want it to have?

252

Which particular person that you've lost contact with would you most like to surprise with a phone call this Christmas?

253

What is the greatest extreme you've ever gone to in order to get someone a particular Christmas gift?

254

If you could take a scenic drive anywhere in America this holiday season, where would you most want to drive?

255

In the song "The Twelve Days of Christmas," how many gifts would one receive if you added up all of the gifts given in every verse from day one to day twelve?

256

What is your best explanation for children of how Santa can fit down a chimney? What if there is no chimney?

257

Y ou, your family, and your friends are trapped in your home for three days following a Christmas Eve blizzard. What would you do to keep everyone entertained and retain a sense of peace in the house?

258

I f you were caught in the act of opening one of your Christmas presents before Christmas, what excuse would you be likely to give?

259

What's the best use you can think of for snow?

260

Suppose you were the cruise director for a riverboat making a Christmas cruise down the Mississippi River. What would you do to make this four-hour dinner cruise a Christmas event that all the passengers would remember?

261

Suppose you were one of ten individuals randomly selected to do some Christmas caroling. On a scale of one to ten (with one being the best singer and ten being the worst), how do you think your singing ability would rank relative to the other people in the group?

262

If you were going to create your own greeting cards this holiday season, what would you do to make them unique?

263

If you were an airline pilot with a plane full of passengers at 12:00 A.M. on Christmas Day, what might you do (or have your crew do) to make the arrival of Christmas Day special?

264

If you could cover any large area with ice *besides* a body of water, what would you want to ice over?

265

When was the last time you decorated a Christmas tree on Christmas Eve?

266

If you could decorate a tree in your house for another holiday besides Christmas, what holiday would it be?

267

If you made music boxes for your living, what one really unique box would you introduce for this Christmas season?

268

What is one thing you will do this Christmas that you were unable to do or attend last Christmas?

269

If you had to miss your family's Christmas celebration (such as hanging the stockings, Christmas dinner, opening gifts, trimming the tree, etc.), which part would you miss the most?

270

Would you rather receive a puppy or a kitten as a Christmas gift?

271

Have you ever secretly communicated your Christmas gift preference to someone? How did you do it?

272

If you were the president of a large corporation and could give only one type of gift to your 1,000 employees, what would it be?

273

If you could hire a skywriter to write a special Christmas message in the sky over your city or town, what would it be?

274

What's the greatest distance you've ever traveled in order to take part in a Christmas celebration?

275

If you kept a journal of Christmases, which year's Christmas would have the lengthiest entry?

276

Have you ever begun a friendship or romance with someone on Christmas?

277

Have you ever opened someone else's present by mistake?

278

What color do you think Santa's hair was before it turned white?

279

Have you ever written a letter to Santa? Did you get an answer back?

280

What's your favorite day of the week for Christmas to fall on?

281

Who is the oldest person you've ever celebrated Christmas with?

282

What room in your house has the least number of decorations at Christmas?

283

Once Christmas has come and gone, are you the type that wants spring to arrive as fast as possible?

284

You're the editor of a general-interest magazine. What will you put on the cover of your Christmas issue?

285

What movie's Christmas celebration would you most like to have attended?

286

Whats your preferred method of displaying Christmas cards, if you display them at all?

287

If you had to receive the same gift each year, what would you want it to be?

288

If you had to give the same gift to every person on your Christmas list, what would it be?

289

What's the largest Christmas Day (or Christmas Eve) gathering you've ever attended?

290

What's the first Christmas song you remember learning?

291

If you were a department store Santa, which aspects of the job would you enjoy the most?

292

What's the biggest change in your life since last Christmas?

293

If money were no object, would you hire a personal shopper to do your Christmas shopping for you?

294

Have you ever "recycled" a Christmas gift?

295

If you could receive any new Christmas ornament this holiday season, what would you like it to be?

296

Have you ever had a present destroyed by an inquisitive (or hungry) pet?

297

What's the warmest Christmas you can remember?

298

In your opinion, what would the ideal centerpiece look like for a holiday dinner in your home? Describe it in detail.

299

What do you do with your Christmas cards after the holidays are over?

300

If snow could somehow fall and accumulate in a warm climate, would you enjoy it more?

301

As the end of the year approaches, it's only natural to reflect back on the last twelve months. Which three news events would you label as the most memorable of the year?

If you were hosting a Christmas party and had to choose one question in this book to use as an icebreaker with your guests, which one would you choose?

About the Authors

BRET NICHOLAUS and PAUL LOWRIE are 1991 graduates of Bethel College, St. Paul, Minnesota. They hold their degrees in public relations/advertising and marketing, respectively. Both authors are firmly committed to providing positive entertainment for adults and children alike.